C000205085

CHARLIE HAMMOND'S
SKETCH-BOOK

Charlie Hammond's Sketch-Book

Introduced by
Christopher Fry

Oxford New York Toronto
OXFORD UNIVERSITY PRESS
1980

Oxford University Press, Walton Street, Oxford OX2 6DP

Oxford London Glasgow
New York Toronto Melbourne Wellington
Kuala Lumpur Singapore Hong Kong Tokyo
Delhi Bombay Calcutta Madras Karachi
Nairobi Dar Es Salaam Cape Town

British Library Cataloguing in Publication Data

Hammond, Charlie
Charlie Hammond's sketch book.
1. Australia — Social life and customs
2. New Zealand — Social life and customs
I. Title
994.03'092'4 DU107 80-40605

ISBN 0-19-212974-0

Printed in Hong Kong by
Bright Sun Printing Press Co. Ltd.

The frontispiece illustration shows Charlie Hammond
in his studio in Dandenong, near Melbourne

INTRODUCTION

On 15 February 1870 my grandparents, Emma and Rowland Hammond, were entertaining to supper, at 41 Milner Square, Islington, Emma's brother Charles Edward Fry, his wife 'Kitty' and their two sons. Before the end of the evening Emma found that another event was about to take over. At 11.25 that night Charles Edward Bruges Hammond was born, named Charles Edward after his uncle at the supper table, and Bruges after another of his mother's brothers. He was the eighth child born of the marriage, preceded by four girls and three boys. They were Ada, Bessie, Percy, Edith, Helen (known as Lil), Bert or Bertie, and Harry Beaumont, known as Hal. The family up to now had been moderately prosperous, my grandfather Rowland following in his father's footsteps as auctioneer and estate agent, but my mother told me he also played the Stock Exchange unwisely and tried to balance his accounts by gambling on cards and horses. By the time my mother, 'Daisy', was born, twenty months after Charlie, on 13 November 1871, the family finances had begun to be unsteady, and by New Year's Day 1873 the servants had all gone and the house in Milner Square had been sold. For a year the family managed uncomfortably in lodgings, moving three times before Rowland got a job in Leamington Spa and settled, if that is the word, his family in a rented house there in Milverton Crescent. This was where

Charlie's memories, when he came to illustrate them in his sketch-books, begin, as I tell in the book I wrote about my family's history, *Can You Find Me*.

But 1875 came in with what seems to have been another crisis. At any rate on 29 January they made a hasty move from Milverton Crescent to Rugby Road. 'Ada, Bertie and Charlie ill but with Hal went in a fly to the new house. The others walking & Daisy in her pram. Wet day.' Things went from bad to worse. Eighteen months later the family fled back to London, staying with relations and friends until, on 30 June 1876, they came to the last family home they would have, 22 Somerville Road, New Cross, which the children called Some Vile Road, with good reason as time soon began to show. It was where my grandmother Emma's long illness began, ending with her death in 1885; where grandfather Rowland took to drink and became such a problem that a separation was arranged, and from where, in July 1881, he departed for Australia.

Rowland's parents and sisters, and Emma's parents and brothers, did what they could to make life easier. The Hammonds had a summer home in Yorkshire, Raven Hall, near Scarborough, at which the grandchildren spent occasional holidays; and the Frys (Emma's family) lived at a house called Springfield, in the village of Winscombe,

Somerset. The first picture in this selection from the sketch-books shows the young Charlie painting a picture of the house, with his grandfather Thomas Homfray Fry in the doorway. Later in life, after the many adventures shown in this book, when he had bought himself some uncleared land in Victoria, he built himself a home and named it, after his grandfather's village, Winscombe. The driveway he cut through the bush, at Tecoma on the outskirts of Melbourne, is now known as Winscombe Avenue.

A third house where holidays were sometimes spent during the time at Somerville Road was St. Mary's Fields, Leicester. One of my grandfather Rowland's sisters, Augusta Hammond, known as Gussie, married Willie Bates, much loved by his nephew-and-nieces-in-law. He was the owner of a rubber factory, and built St. Mary's Fields not far from the factory and the canal which served it. There were two children of the marriage, Altie and Katie, and when my mother was twelve she went to live at St. Mary's Fields, to be a companion for Katie. It was here that she spent her teens, and here that Charlie joined her for a blissful year (1888-9) after his first adventurous year in the antipodes.

Life in Some Vile Road was a struggle, waged with patience and courage by Emma. The two older boys, Bert and Hal, were at school at Haberdashers Aske's, paid for by their uncles (Percy was already married and living in Staffordshire); Charlie was sent to the Technical and Commercial Schools in south London. Bert was already showing some skill in drawing and painting. Hal drew, too, but with a cruder talent. Their sister Ada wrote in her diary in 1880: 'Hal is decorating envelopes with comic drawings in Indian ink and selling them for pocket money.' Charlie also was busy with his pencil. I possess a childish, but confident, drawing of a horse which he made at Leamington when he was five or six years old. When he was fourteen, the year before he set sail for New Zealand, he was awarded the South Kensington certificate for freehand and model drawing at his school's prize-giving day. Emma, before she married, had drawn and painted very pleasantly, as her mother had done before her. Some of their pictures have come down to me and also a little water-colour of the house in Milverton Crescent, done by Emma's brother Charles Edward Fry.

For two years after my grandfather had left them and gone to Australia the family held together as best they could. The first to adventure into the unknown was Hal. In 1883, when he was sixteen, he set sail for Canada, with no friends or contacts there, and scarcely any money. How he nearly died of typhoid as soon as he arrived, his fight for survival, and enlistment into the North-West Mounted Police, is told in *Can You Find Me*.

The second to go was Bert, far less suited to any kind of adventure than Hal was; nerve-wracked and constantly plagued by ill-health, somewhat scorned by Hal but loved by his young brother Charlie. He set sail for Australia in a three-master on 12 April 1884, and was met at Adelaide by his father. Five days before he sailed his sister Ada had written in her diary: 'Edith home & almost immediately commenced the startling news that she & Lil wished to go to New Zealand.' They left England two months later, leaving Emma at Some Vile Road with the two eldest, Ada and Bessie, and fourteen-year-old Charlie. Hal's letters home stirred him to thoughts of following his brother to Canada. He wrote asking whether carpentry would be a useful preparation for life in the North-West Territory. He was good with his hands, had made himself a photographic camera in the school laboratory and won a prize for 'magnetism and electricity'. But at the end of October 1884 Hal had despaired of making a living and enlisted for a five-year term in the Mounties. In a letter to his mother he wrote: 'When Skybobblums, alias Charlie, gets old enough, if nothing else turns up, enlist him and he's off your hands.' Skybobblums or Chobblemiss were his nicknames for Charlie, deriving, it would seem, from Charlie's slight stammer on the letter b. But his sister Lil who by now was married to a young man she had met on the boat, had another plan: that Charlie should join them on their sheep farm at Port Underwood across Cook Start from Wellington. On 18 February, 1885, three days after his fifteenth birthday, a berth was booked for him on the *Arawa*, leaving for New Zealand on 26 March. Emma was too ill to see him off – she had only six more months to live – but his sister Bessie went with him to Tilbury, and reported to her mother when she got home that he had already made friends with another boy who was also setting off on his own.

After the publication of *Can You Find Me* I found, tucked away between the pages of one of Charlie's sketchbooks, the letter that Emma wrote to him the next morning:

March 27th

My own dear Boy

Although I am not yet well enough to write you a long letter, I must tell you how delighted I was on Bessie's return home to hear that you had a companion whom I could feel sure would guide you aright, and prove the true friend I so longed for you to have . . . . I so much wish I could have seen your good kind friend that I might picture you together. How I hope you will be somewhat of a companion to him during such a long voyage. I believe I have made the great mistake in thinking you would go the same way as the girls did, and find you are going by the Cape of Good Hope, therefore perhaps you will not see such wonderful things as they did and yet perhaps enough to make some sketches of . . . . I thought of you a great deal during the night and wondered if you had found your bedding & how you would sleep for the first time in a bunk. God bless and keep you my boy till you reach your new home, and sometimes give a thought to the old Mother left behind.

Charlie did find enough on the voyage to make sketches of, and went on to record in pictures the adventures he had, and the places he saw, during the rest of his long life. Often he copied one and sent it with a letter to my mother, in a loving correspondence which lasted for more than sixty years. When I was married his wedding present to us was a sepia water-colour painting, copied and enlarged from his sketch-books, of Uncle Willie and Aunt Gussie Bates, with their daughter Katie and my mother, driving in their carriage through the gates of St. Mary's Fields, Altie Bates and Charlie on horseback beside them, a memory of the year 1888. My mother had told me that, in a letter to her, Charlie said he was going to leave the sketch-books to me when he died. The time came and passed; indeed it was some time after his death that we heard of his dying. In 1959, or thereabouts, I wrote to cousins in Australia asking about the sketch-books. They had no knowledge of them. And then Adza Vincent, who was helping me with secretarial work, suggested that she should write to anyone whom Charlie mentioned in his last letters. Eventually we found the sketch-books were in the keeping of a neighbour, Mrs Milner (now Mrs Beanland), who wrote saying she thought my uncle would like me to have them. Since it was by her care of them that the books had survived I felt I should buy them from her, and they were crated up and flown to England, ten large sketch-books full not only of his drawings but also press-cuttings, letters, photographs, and mementoes hoarded from his childhood and boyhood and kept through all his wanderings.

After the tragic self-slaughter of Bert in 1904 Charlie wrote an inscription on the first page of the third sketch-book which shall stand, as he would have wished if he had ever thought the drawings would be published, as a dedication to this book:

TO my dear big brother Bert who has shown so much sympathy and taken so much interest in my welfare from early childhood; who has influenced my life more than anyone else; who first taught me to tell the time by the clock and East from West by the compass; who gave me my first lessons in art, photography and other useful studies; who shared with me many happy hopeful days before the collapse of the land-boom in Melbourne 1893 and battled through the years of the depression which followed. To him I affectionately dedicate these books of our adventure through life.

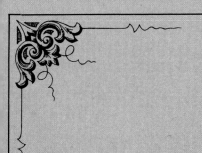

THE SKETCH-BOOK

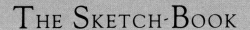

I
Early Days in England

The date (1880) which Charlie put to the painting of Springfield, his grandfather Fry's house in Winscombe, is certainly wrong. His grandfather had died in November 1878. His grandmother died in August 1879, and his mother took him down to Winscombe for the funeral. His great-aunt Mary Anna Fry wrote to my mother: 'How glad you will be to see your dear Mamma home again. Your little brother seems to be enjoying himself here how quiet he is, I could not hear a word he said.' He evidently painted a picture of the house during that visit, and added an earlier memory of his grandfather in the doorway. The Christmas pictures on the next page are something of a puzzle, too. The portico with the maid in cap and apron, the grand bed and the Christmas dinner have the appearance of St. Mary's Fields, Leicester, not of the austerities of Leamington or Somerville Road, but I have no record of a childhood Christmas at Leicester. It seems to be a fantasy picture, and fact begins with the snowballing in London. Peckham Rye, where he played in the cricket-match, was where both the Hammonds and the Frys were living when Emma first met Rowland in 1849. His first taste of seafaring was a rough one; he was too seasick to write home for some time; but he had his sketch-book at the ready for the life ahead.

GRANDPA FRY'S HOME
"WINSCOMBE"
MENDIP HILLS, SOMERSET.
1880

C.H.

CHRISTMAS EVE

THE WAITS

"SANTA CLAWS"

CHRISTMAS MORNING.

A MERRY CHRISTMAS

A HAPPY CHRISTMAS AND A BRIGHT NEW YEAR

CHRISTMAS SERVICE
HARK! THE HERALD ANGELS SING.

DAISY & I SURVEY THE XMAS DINNER.
PROSPECTS OF A GOOD TIME.

C.H. GOING TO SCHOOL IN LONDON.
Return to London from Leamington 1878.

AT WORK IN THE LABORATORY
MAKING MY FIRST PHOTOGRAPHIC CAMERA. 1883.

"MY PETS"

SKATING ON BLACKHEATH POND 1883.
C.H.

C.H. at the wickets.   MATCH ON PECKHAM RYE.   1884.

CYCLING THROUGH THE GREEN LANES OF ENGLAND

LAST EVENINGS IN OLD HOME.

BREAKING UP THE HOME.

One by one my brothers & sisters had left the old nest to seek
their fortunes in foreign lands; Bert to Australia; Hal to Canada;
Edith & Lil to New Zealand; Perce & Daisy to Staffordshire & Leicester so
only Ada, Bess & myself remained with mother.

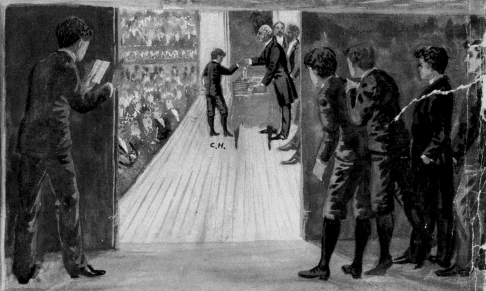

C.H.

DISTRIBUTION OF SCHOOL PRIZES BY THE LORD MAYOR OF LONDON.
RECEIVING 5TH KENSINGTON CERTIFICATE FOR FREEHAND & MODEL DRAWING, MAGNETISM
ELECTRICITY

MARCH 25TH 1885. BID MOTHER AND HOME GOOD BYE.
"IT MAY BE FOR YEARS,— IT MAY BE FOR EVER."

Bess came down to Tilbury to see me off aboard the "Arawa" at 5 pm on March 25th 1885. The last whistle blew, friends & relatives were parked & the big ship steamed slowly down the muddy Thames and dear old smoky London, the land of our birth disappeared gradually from view.

SHAW, SAVILLE & ALBION COS SS. ARAWA. 5200 TONS, 3500 H.P.

The first night at sea was very dark, bitterly cold & blowing hard, everything was strange about me; strange faces, strange noises; The pains in my inside were particularly strange.

II
A NEW LIFE IN NEW ZEALAND

Charlie had forgotten his seasickness by the time the *Arawa* reached Port Chalmers: and his homesickness was lost in the delight of landing on the quarantine island (the ship's cook had developed smallpox during the voyage). But Lil's husband, Robert Staveley, had given up sheep-farming at Port Underwood and gone into partnership with a solicitor called Monteith. Charlie was put to work with a shipping-agency, Heaton and Miller, in Wellington. Three months later he was sent to Auckland to live with his sister Edith, who had married her cousin Frank Hammond junior. He was homesick again, though sometimes at weekends he got away from his disciplinarian sister to stay with his uncle, Frank Hammond senior, and enjoyed the friendship of his young cousins. As Edith was expecting her first child, he was lodged with a family called Davis. 'Aunt Rebecca', whose grave can be seen from Cemetery Bridge, was Frank Hammond senior's first wife. Shaken by the news of the death of his mother, Charlie escaped from the dull life of an office-boy and, after a spell as cabin-boy on the SS *Minnie Casey*, joined the crew of a brigantine bound for Melbourne.

ARRIVAL AT CAPE TOWN.

On Wedy 15th April. There was unusual excitement on board for we were nearing land which we sighted for the first time since leaving England. and on Thursday morning we steamed into the harbour of Cape Town

on Monday 4th May, we arrived at Hobart after a record passage of 38 days from London

ARAWA

C.H.

on Wedy 6th May. We steam into Port Chalmers NZ. but having smallpox aboard we are landed on the quarantine island. I shall never forget my first glimpse of Maori land. The weather was bright & mild; no one had been on the island for years. the wild tropical foliage & highly coloured birds; everything so peaceful & sublime, surpassed all my wildest expectations and was happy all the time fishing or wandering about through the forest.

on Thursday 14th we set foot ashore on the main land. a great crowd assembled on the wharf to witness the landing of the "new chums" Port Chalmers was a small & primitive looking place after London

ARRIVAL AT WELLINGTON.

I had look'd forward all the voyage to the pleasant times I expected to have on Lil's sheep run I had dreamed of green hills; flocks of fat sheep; wild fruit; ponies to ride &c, but when Lil met me on the wharf & told me they had given up the sheep run, It was the greatest disappointment I had ever had.

LIL'S HOME AT POLLHILL GULLY, MITCHELTOWN. (Mrs Robert Jones Staveley).

However Lil's home was prettily situated on the hills of Mitcheltown. Wellington & I soon overcame my great disappointment

HARBOUR OF WELLINGTON. MAY. 1885.

The main portion of the town is hidden by the hill in the foreground. On the right the cliffs are being cut away to fill in part of the harbour for building on; the railway shown was employed in carrying the stone tipping it into the bay.

AUGst 27th 1885. Leave Wellington for Auckland aboard the USSC^{os} PENGUIN.

EDITHS HOUSE. VIEW ROAD MT EDEN AUCKLAND. 1885.

SUGAR WORKS.

UNCLE FRANKS

BIRKENHEAD

North cote

Ferryboat

NORTH SHORE.

Rangitoto.

OLD MILL.

QUEEN STREET WHARF

ALBERT PARK

K HOSPITAL.

BAY VIEW R^d

Domain.

MT EDEN.

AUCKLAND FROM MT EDEN 1885.

SEP. 1ST 1885. START IN THE OFFICE OF JNO MILNE
ACCOUNTANT & AUDITOR, QUEEN ST

EDITH CLARA

←the Criminal. C.H.

Always in trouble. If I'm not doing something
I'm doing something else (as paddy would say)
Forgot to open bedroom window; left a collar on the bed;
Did not bath enough. Came into house with boots on &c.

HOMESICK.
"Taking one thing with another my life is
not a happy one." (with Edith)

C.H. BOB   KATE GUSSIE.

UNCLE FRANK HAMMOND'S HOME, NORTHCOTE (ACROSS THE BAY)

C.H.

GATHERING HONEY & BIRDS NESTS
WITH ARTHUR & ROLLIE.

NOVR 1885.   I GO TO LIVE WITH DAVIS' SEAVIEW RD. MᵗEDEN

AUNT REBECCA'S GRAVE

THE CEMETERY BRIDGE.
MY NEW WAY TO THE OFFICE.

SKETCHING IN AUCKLAND DOMAIN.
NEAR MY NEW HOME.

One day, as I sat alone in the office with a fearful headache from working over books, my thoughts drifted back to England and Mother. I wondered how long it would be before I saved enough to return home & make her happy for the rest of her days. How different things had turned out to what I had expected.

I was aroused by the postman's knock. A letter for me with deep black border. — It was news of Mother's death! All I seemed to have been living for had gone.

Rollie

Psalm Singing
Slave driving Uncle Frank

Arthur

Bob

C H

MY 16TH BIRTHDAY. SURVEYING & CUTTING ROADS THROUGH THE BUSH.

My Uncle was a very religious man but nevertheless a slave driver. and after keeping us working from early morning till late at night. stood over us while we pitched our tent & did a lot of useless work like clearing scrub around it. although we were dead tired.

C H

Arthur.

We are at last allowed to turn in. Arthur falls asleep before he gets into bed. last man in blows out the light.

We are just comfortably asleep & warm when a sudden & terrific storm strikes the tent & carries it sky high & we are left out in the wide, wide world

So scrambling into our clothes we make tracks for the house through the blinding rain & wind. falling over logs. bumping into trees & groping in the darkness. we arrive at last wet cold & hungry & dead tired. so ended my 16th birthday.

Arthur

CH

Bob

Rollie

CH in Church

It took Uncle all his time to keep us boys in order. He never had such a time before. every chance we got, we slipped off through the bush down to the bay where we spent the days pleasantly swimming; gathering oisters & other shell fish, kiakau, Maori potatoes &c &cooking them on a log fire; making shafts & having all sorts of fun.

on sundays, I loved to wander through the glorious forest (natures great Cathedral) & listen to the the feathered choristers singing their praises to God. It seemed to take me nearer to Heaven than sitting in a stuffy weatherboard structure, listening to the same prayers & hymns that I had heard hundreds of times before, repeated in a parrot like manner; but my Uncle, who was the local preacher, did not agree with me and I was set down as a very bad boy.

"THE LAST BOAT for Auckland"

Northhead   Rangitoto

Midnight.   Queen St Wharf.
               Auckland.
Feeling very sorry for myself.

Commencing Life at the bottom of the tree.
Mt EDEN 2 A.M.   Look out for the softest place to lie on
                    and the softest stone for a pillow.

One of the most comical, yet pitiable sights, was the ladies cabin in bad weather. I would go in to see if they were all right and on opening the door, I would see a confused mass of blankets, rugs, jugs, basins, bottles and women rolling from side to side.

I soon became famous throughout the district, for my sketches; all hands, from the skipper to cabin boy, came in for a share of glorious caricaturing.

"MY 'FIRST THEATRE" KAIPARA. N.Z.
I did not like to look (except through my fingers). I thought she had forgotten to finish dressing."

I was very fond of exploring the upper reaches of the rivers miles away from Civilisation. On one occasion I found a great log stuck in the centre of the stream, so I pulled alongside & climbed on it, but forgot to make my boat fast so when I looked round it had drifted downstream. I could not swim & the current was too strong to attempt it, yet I might stay on a week or month before anyone would find me. So I had the choice of staying on the log and starving or jumping in & getting drowned but providence was watching over me again (as she does over all silly fools). I saw the boat touch the bank, then slowly turn past the log but close to the shore, it was in a backwash. I anxiously watched it drift out into mid stream & come right up to meet me as if it had been carefully steered.

III

ADVENTURES AT SEA, AND
RETURN TO THE OLD HOME

Bert was working for an interior decorator called Mouncey in Melbourne. Much as Charlie delighted in Bert's company his thoughts were set on getting back to England. He found an American ship bound for Hong Kong, and had a tough time of it as one of a largely shanghaied crew. At Hong Kong he was taken on by a ship sailing to England. After meeting with his sisters Ada and Bessie in London (Bessie took him to see his mother's grave) and getting his discharge papers at Liverpool, he was invited by Willie and Gussie Bates to join my mother at St. Mary's Fields, Leicester. These were happy days he never forgot. He was apprenticed to a farmer, Mr Warren, and made friends with a high-spirited young man called Will Payne (they can be seen both riding on one horse). After a visit to Buffalo Bill's circus in London he became expert at knife-throwing, roping, and trick-shooting. But he was still restless for adventure, and when a letter came from Bert in February 1889, full of enthusiasm about a block of land he had bought at Sandringham, a Melbourne suburb, and enclosing a drawing of the dream-house he meant to build there, Charlie decided to join him. 'Come and help me build my shanty and act captain of the yacht and we can do the Robinson Crusoe and Friday tip-top,' Bert wrote. Uncle Tom Fry, with whom he played tennis at Blackheath before sailing, was Emma's youngest brother. He worked his passage as steward on the Melbourne-bound *Riverina*.

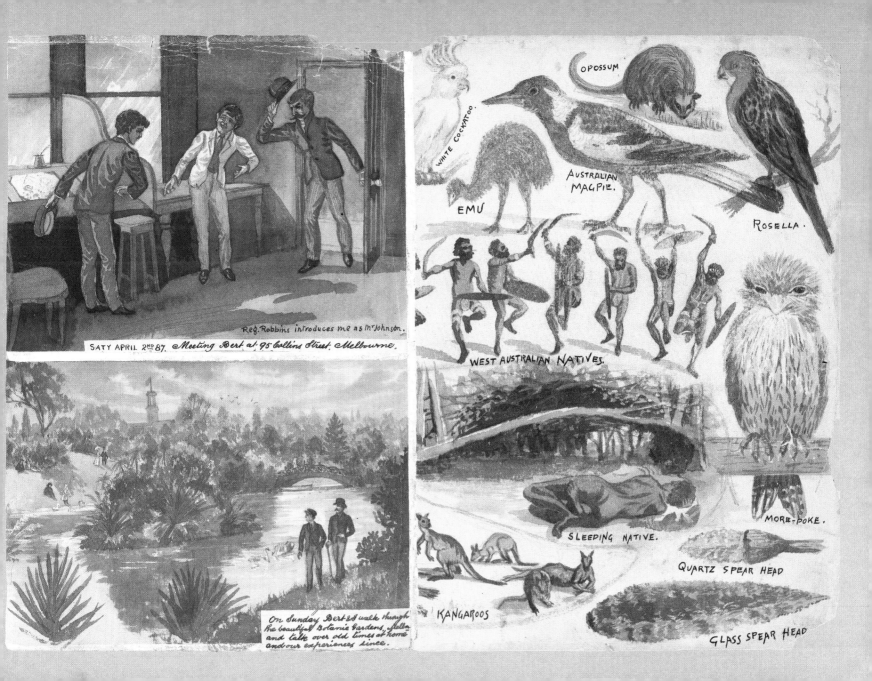

Reg. Robbins introduces me as Mr Johnson.

SATY APRIL 2ND 87. Meeting Bert at 95 Collins Street. Melbourne.

On Sunday Bert & I walk through the beautiful Botanic Gardens, Melb. and talk over old times at home and our experiences since.

WHITE COCKATOO.

OPOSSUM

EMU

AUSTRALIAN MAGPIE.

ROSELLA.

WEST AUSTRALIAN NATIVES.

MORE-POKE.

SLEEPING NATIVE.

KANGAROOS

QUARTZ SPEAR HEAD

GLASS SPEAR HEAD

The Ship "Great Admiral" at Sandridge. (Pt MELBn) Ap. 27th 1887.
"What Ship Jack!"? The runner from the "All Nations" takes me in tow.

Saturday night. Shanghaing the Crew of the Boston Ship Great Admiral from the All Nations The notorious boarding house once known to every sailor as The Chausan.

Ap. 1887.
At 4 bells (2 o'clock) Sunday morning. Straightening out the Crew. The mates Knock "8 bells" out of the drugged crew.
"The mate was a great "pick me up".

Sunday morning, 5 bells. Heave up the anchor.
(2.30 A.M.)

"ALL'S WELL!"
Lookout on the fo'cas'le head.

Fore-upper-top's'l carries away

SHORT OF WATER — Drinking rain water off the decks during a heavy storm in the China seas.

COLD COMFORT.

We spend an awful time aloft in the pitch darkness with the wind howling and blowing through the rigging & the rain pouring down in icy cold torrents. We retire for our disturbed sleep, wet, cold, hungry & exhausted. Turn out on deck with nothing to eat or drink to warm us.

"THE MUTINY" — The mates brutality & tyranny at last aroused the sailors to desperation. one day he was cursing a German sailor for not being quick enough & giving him a kick & a push, ordered him on the fo'c's'l head. The man waited until he reached the top of the ladder & the mate followed. Then, turning round, hit the mate fair in eye and rocked him down on the deck below, then jumped on him. The crew seized the opportunity & drawing their knives rushed in to finish him off & throw him overboard but the second mate, bosun and bosun's mate kept them off until the skipper hearing the commotion rushed up with his rifle & soon scattered the mutineers. Instead of all being put in irons, the skipper sympathised with the men, the German sailor had easy times for the remainder of the voyage.

SOLOMAN ISLAND NATIVES.

HOMEWARD BOUND, ALONG NARBRO ROAD.

Arrival at Leicester from Liverpool.
Daisy drives in to meet me.
Oct. 1887.

A hearty welcome to St Mary's Fie
Oct. 1887.

St. MARYS FIELDS.   1887.

K.
D.
ALT.
CH

A pleasant evening in the old nursery. Distributing curios from foreign parts.   My beautiful bedroom. What a contrast with the tough life at sea!

reakfast with Daisy, Katie, Altie and nurse Kettle.
Mowbray pork pies, fresh eggs &c. a striking contrast to salt horse and 49 ers.

After breakfast, the girls drive off to school in Leicester

BACK GARDEN (View from spareroom)
After showing me his favourite hunter and other horses, I strole down with Alt to his office.

and I am left alone for the rest of the day to
wander round & admire the house and gardens at St Mary's
Fields.

ALTIE
ON TOMMY.

First Cub hunt of the season. Cunnard hounds meet at John Ball Covert. There being no other horse in the stable, except carriage horses, fit to follow. I ride Alt's old bicycle to the Meet.

My "horse," never having been schooled over fences, I have to be content to watch the hounds from the road.

"GONE AWAY !!!"
My "horse" creates quite a stir among the followers at the Meet.

C.E.H.   Daisy

St. Mary's Fields. Narborough Road. Leicester. 1887.

St Marys Fields. Leicester 1888.

CRICKET PRACTICE WITH ALT. IN FIELD IN FRONT OF HOUSE.

I WIN AN EXCITING BILLIARD MATCH WITH ALT. FOR A RIFLE.

a sail in the "Ida" with Will Farmer

We have many pleasant sails in Will Farmer's boat.
(St Mary's Fields, on the hill.)

MUSIC IN THE OLD NURSERY. ST MARY'S FIELDS. 1888.
(Gilbert & Sullivan's operas)
NURSE EMILY KETTLE. KATIE. DAISY. ALTIE.

C.H. (Dreaming.
Visions in smoke)

UNCLE WILLIE TURNS TO A PILLAR OF SNOW after his Christmas dinner.

Christmas 1888. St. Marys Fields. Leicester.
Amuse myself and others by modelling Uncle Will & Barry in Snow.

We set traps for Louie Penman (Chamber maid) but every body falls into them but her. Dear Uncle Willie gets a wetting at the old nursery

Our bedroom at 10 p.m.
Six nights a week. Lace pillowslips have a bad time.

CHRISTMAS FESTIVITIES, LEICESTER. 1888.

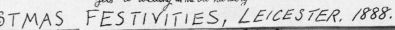

Garner's Fancy dress ball.

Barnetts evening dress ball.

West-field house. back View.   Driving to market jirth the Farmer, W.m Warren, to learn the buying & selling of Cattle & horses &c.

SHEPHERDING WITH W. WARREN. OUTBREAK OF ANTHRAX.

The start of the Anthrax desease in England which ruins Mr Warren.

1ST MEETING OF WILL PAYNE.

In the evening a young fellow rode up on a fiery black Irish pony. It was Will Payne from Hall farm Foston, 3 miles off, we took a great fancy to each other & became fast friends.

Next evening He brought over a gun for me & we went out shooting young rooks which were just beginning to fly & made nice pies.

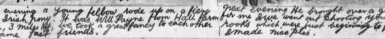

LEICESTER CATTLE MARKET.

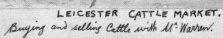

Buying and selling Cattle with Mr Warren.

"THE HORSE FAIR" Leicester.

Buying horses at the Leicester Fair with Mr Warren.

"The last of the White corn. men beat the last
few square yards, dozens of rabbits run out, Will Payne & I have
a lively few minutes shooting not one gets away.

(Peatling Covert in background)

Returning to Hall Farm after the Opera in Leicester.
A nine mile drive on a dark and frosty night.
Contemplating a raid on the pantry and Mrs Payne's
delicious Jam puffs.

Our "nice little Sunday
evening strole".
5 miles through snow in
slippers. Fall into
snowdrift and lose slippers.

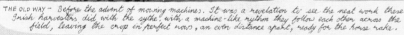

The old Way

THE OLD WAY – Before the advent of mowing machines. It was a revelation to see the neat work these
Irish harvesters did with the sythe. with a machine-like rythom they follow each other across the
field, leaving the crop in perfect rows, an even distance apart, ready for the horse rake.

WARREN

"Billie" Warren up to date:- buys a new mowing machine.

LEICESTER   START FOR THE 5 MILE BICYCLE RACE ON THE TRACK.   C.H.(RED).

BERT GARNER ON HIS SAFETY, MAKES THE PACE A CRACKER.

LAST LAP.   ALT. LEAVES THE FIELD   BEHIND.

I LAY MY EARS BACK, SET MY TEETH AND PUT ON A MIGHTY SPURT. OVERHAUL ALT. AT THE HOMETURN.—

— AND WIN   THE FIVE MILES. PRINCIPAL EVENT OF THE DAY.

My last run with the hounds.
A bad fall on the frosty surface of bridge

May 1889. Good bye to dear old St Mary's Fields and its happy days.
Leave Leicester for London on my return to Australia.

My last game in England, with Uncle Tom Fry. May 1889.
at The Elms. Blackheath. London.

"Hang on Chas!"
If I didn't become a nervous wreck it was no fault of
my Chum Will Payne.

IV
AUSTRALIA

The affection and help which Bert had given to Charlie during their boyhood was renewed. Charlie joined him in Mouncey's interior decorating business, and the lessons in art and photography were taken up again. Bert was becoming an expert at painting portraits of race-horses – 'a *genius* at painting a standing horse', Charlie wrote. 'No other artist could compare with him.' Charlie constructed a front-sliding shutter for the camera, and took some early instantaneous photographs of horse-races. Incidentally, the records show that, in the 1889 Melbourne Cup, Carbine came second and Melos third – not the other way round, as Charlie shows it.

Towards the end of 1889 Hal left Canada and was welcomed by his brothers in Melbourne. They all three settled into a bungalow in Malvern Vale which they named Bachelors' Hall, and then spent a Christmas holiday together in the mountains. Hal encouraged Charlie to play tricks on the nervous Bert (always recognizable by his pointed mustachios). The threesome did not last. Bert and Charlie earned enough now from photography and painting to give up working for Mouncey. They took a studio together in Melbourne. But in 1892 came the collapse of the land-boom. Unemployment was rife. The studio was ransacked, the cameras stolen, and no one could afford to buy paintings. They tried farming, but that, as the drawings show, was no life for Bert. They sold up and set off for New Zealand.

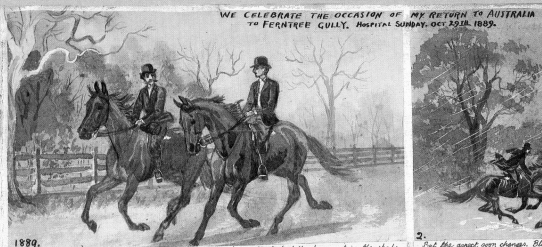

1889.

Bert predicted a most enjoyable ride. "We can start early before the heat of the day, rest in the shady fern gullies and return in the cool of the evening" The sky was cloudless as we started off and threatened to be a hot day so I dressed accordingly. Bert (always a careful man) took precautions to carry a macintosh.

2.

But the aspect soon changes. Black clouds appered and we were caught in a heavy squall. We gallop for the nearest shelter, the Mountain View Hotel, Burwood road, a mile away, where we remain until the rain stops then proceed on our way, Bert quite sure that there would be no more rain that day.

3.

We are soon caught in another squall which is followed by a terrific thunder storm and bitterly cold wind. being wet through, with no shelter for miles, we ride on, our horses floundering and slippeing through the flood waters rushing across the road, until we round the Club Hotel at Lower F.T. Gully and, not feeling like "resting in the cool fern gullies" we head for home along the F.T. Gully road and through Oakleigh, against the piercing wind. We pass the Fernside Bicycle Club struggling against it, occasionally trying to mount and ride but only to be blown off again. (Cautious Bert in his macintosh is the only dry man in the crowd.) Arrive at Malvern half frozen and waterlogged and not likely to forget our ride to the Gully.

The greater portion of my spare time was taken up in the study of photography.
Bert and I in the darkroom. 1890. developing the first negatives of jumping races taken in Melbourne.

Sketch of CAULFIELD RACE COURSE. 1890.

CAULFIELD RACE COURSE. PAST THE STAND. 1890.

VICTORIAN RACING CLUBS SPRING MEETING. FLEMINGTON NOV.ᵗ 3ᵈ 1889.

MELBOURE CUP. 1889.   MELBOURNE CUP 1889 CARBINE.   C.E.H.   E.B.H.
Bravo. 1st Melos 2nd Carbine 3rd.

NOVR
1889. Hal arrives in Melbourne unexpectedly from Canada. Bert & I meet him at Spencer Street Stn. Our first meeting since we were schoolboys in London in 1883 when Hal left home for Canada.

We take him home to our "diggings" where he turns out his boxes of Curious & relates his experiences & adventures in the North West Mounted Police, till the small hours of the morning.

Strangely enough Edith also arrives unexpectedly from Hamilton. This was our first meeting since I left her in Auckland. NZ in 1885.

BERT. EDITH & JESSIE.   C.H.   H.B.H.
alias
(Mr Johnson)

We celebrate the occasion by a trip to Ferntree Gully. Where Hal makes himself known to Edith & gives her a great surprise. Hal gets his first experience of an Australian Buck Jumper.

Edith
& Jessie.   Chas.   Bert.   Hal.
(Mr Johnson)

Refreshment at the old Bay View Hotel.
Edith thinks that "Mr Johnson" is something like her brother Hal.
NOV. 1889.

Coo-wee

Leaving Batchelors' Hall for our Christmas holidays in the mountains.

On the road (the contents of the) waggon

A rest by the way. Hal is left to take care of the waggon & stores. He takes particularly good care of some of the pudding and other good things in our absence.

E B H   CH   H B H.

Our first Camp at Healesville
E. B. H. bringing in the lost dog "Batch".

Our Camp by the Watts River. Fernshaw.
Bert spends all his time clearing out the waggon to make a comfortable bed while Hal & I enjoy ourselves over the camp fire.

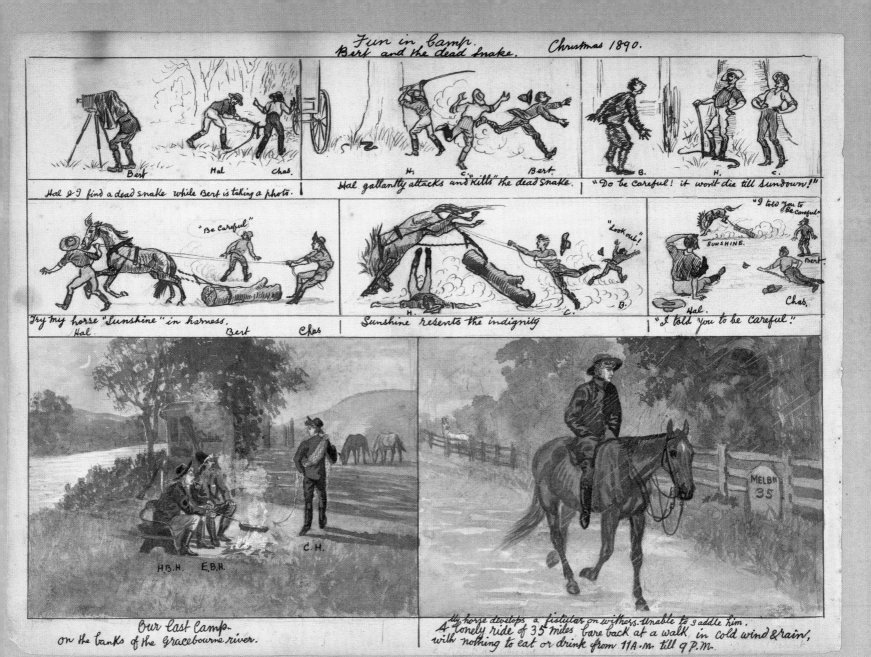

At Batchelors Hall

"By the misty moonbeams straggling light
And the lantern dimly burning."

JUNE 1891. Bert and I make plans for the future. decide
to leave Hal at Batchelors' Hall and go into town,
open a studio and paint portraits of racehorses, hunters &c.

In their endeavour to solve the mystery of Who and What we were,
the Village maidens decide to satisfy their curiosity by giving us a
Surprise Party, but the news leaks out and it ends in a much Surprised Party
and we still remained a mystery.

C.H.   Hal.

Batchelors' Hall.   Hal and I improve our shooting by
target practice & shooting spiders on the walls at meal time.

1891   AT CANTEBURY PARK. (Owners up.)
Dear old Sunshine creates a sensation and a surprise among the amateur
riders.

Burglaries and Suicides were every day occurances after the Boom burst.

Bert

Chas.

We find the back door of our premises open.

Chas.

Bert

I ascend the stairs expecting to see flash from revolver any second.

Bert.

"They've been drinking our health Bert."

LOOKING FOR BURGLARS ON THE ROOF

A SMART ARREST.

A smart arrest was effected last night by Detectives Macmnamy and Ward, and Detective Roach, of Sydney. Whilst on an errand of criminal investigation, they saw standing in a dark spot near the Trades Hall, about 10 o'clock, a young man who was engaged in a confidential conversation with another person. The officers accosted the suspect, but he violently resisted any approach towards him. However, Detective Macmnamy alone soon subdued him, and there were taken from his pockets a six chambered revolver, fully loaded, a number of skeleton keys, a "jemmy," a new necktie and a pocket handkerchief. There was thus ample justification for his apprehension, and he was forthwith placed in the City watchhouse. He gave the name of Bertram Toombs, and his age as 21 years. He will be brought before the City magistrates this morning to give an explanation for having such a dangerous collection in his possession. The officers hope to be able to connect him with some of the burglaries which have recently been committed in and around the city. It was certainly an opportune arrest.

Sunday 6th Nov. 1892.   Return at 10 p.m. after evening with friends and find our studio ransacked by burglars.   Cutting from the "Age."

1. Bert & I go out to the farm and bring waggon to Melbourne.

2. "on the road" We buy horsefeed on our way to town.

3. Loading up at the Studio all day. Exhausted after weeks of packing up.

4. We start off on our long journey. 40 miles on wet and cold night. Harness breaks!

5 & 6. "Jewel" through Richmond. "Jewel" proves herself true to name. Jewel unable to pull the heavy load up hills. Bert goes to Malvern by train to fetch other mare. I have a long and anxious wait in the cold & rain.

7. Put up at Ayres for the night. His yard a foot deep in liquid mud!

8. A hearty welcome at Malvern.

9. We start on our 40 mile trip next day. An incident on the Dandenong road.

10. Expecting to sight the lights of Cranbourne every minute when "B" discovers by the aid of a match that we are 3 miles away yet & 12 more miles to travel.

11. 6 miles from our journeys end, the waggon sinks up to the axles in mud & the mares are unable to shift it.

12. We abandon the load for the night & finish the last 4 miles on foot through the floods. Lose the mares.

13. what Bert declared he saw in the old hut. COW Moo! RATS TARANTULAS & Squeekes BERT. GREAT SNAKES. After Searching for the mares and finding them We stagger on to the farm at 2 A.M. Attend to the horses and fall asleep dead tired in the old hut.

14. It takes us all next day to finish the last 4 miles of our journey & pull the dray out.

15. In the evening I drive Clisby to Cranbourne in a terrific thunder storm. Bert & I are in charge of the farm.

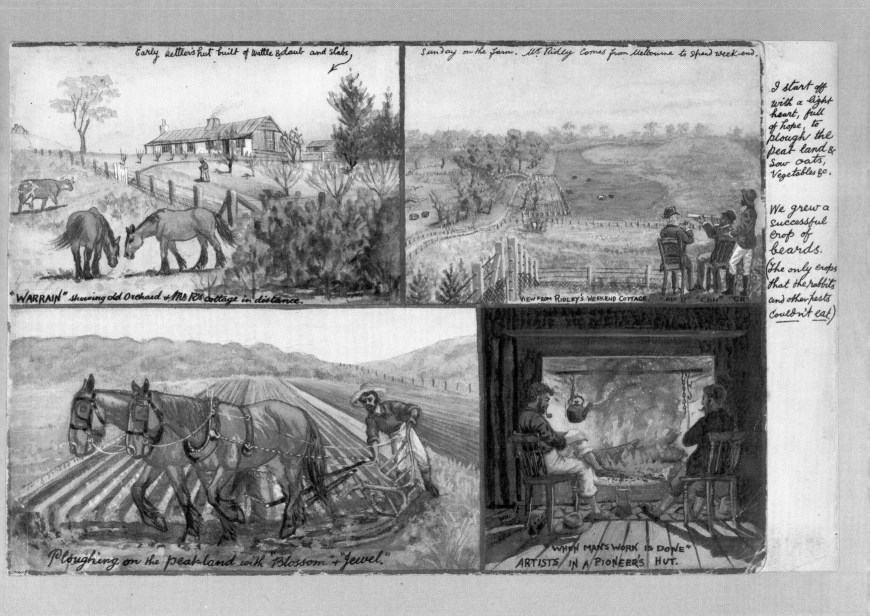

Early settler's hut built of wattle & daub and slabs.

Sunday on the Farm. Mr Ridley comes from Melbourne to spend week-end.

"WARRAIN" showing old Orchard & Mr R's cottage in distance.

VIEW FROM RIDLEY'S WEEKEND COTTAGE.   "MR R"   "EBH"   "CH"

I start off with a light heart, full of hope, to plough the peat land & sow oats, vegetables &c.

We grew a successful crop of beards. (The only crops that the rabbits and other pests couldn't eat.)

Ploughing on the peat-land with "Blossom" & "Jewel."

"WHEN MAN'S WORK IS DONE"
ARTISTS IN A PIONEER'S HUT.

The most successful
Crops we grew were
whiskers. the rabbits
didn't eat them.

Parrots, Magpies
& various pests.

Sowing our wild oats

Mond 28th Aug. 93. We broadcast the last of our Capital (all that the
burglars & hard times have left us) upon the soil — Oh! what will the
harvest be? —— Some fell by the wayside & the parrots came
& chewed them up — some fell on good ground — those
the rabbits got!

Kookaburras.

Riding to Langwarren
for mail.

Round goes the world,
& Trouble I defy,
While jogging along together my boys,
That old grey mare & I.

C.H. on Dolly.

The old mare opens all the gates, the rest follow.

C.H.

LAUGHING
JACKASSES

"BESSIE"
IN THE KITCHEN
GARDEN.

GEESE

"Dolly."

JINNIE

PRETTY POLLY

"The Crop"
Prospects of a good Harvest (for the rabbits)

Work and Fun on the Farm. We get a lot of fun out of life in spite of hard times.

E.B.H. thinks farming a grand opportunity for wearing out his old cloths, but gets a terrible fright when fashionable visitors from Melbourne arrive unexpectedly — E.B.H. off to change!

Our picnic party at the bluff.

Mrs Waller
C.H.
E.B.H.
Ted Waller.

Canvas and Paper off wall of Melb. Studio

E.B.H.

SAILING OUR BOAT ROUND TO THE "BLUFF" IN A 15 KNOT BREEZE, FOR THE AMUSEMENT OF VISITORS. LEAKS LIKE A SIEVE.— E.B.H. MANS THE PUMPS.

AT THE BLUFF.

An oar for a mast with hessian and wallpaper for a sail. Bert bails to windward and gets it in the neck.

Fun on the beach.

Fun on the farm.

Bert's pet pig

Bert sees nothing in milking but what he can do!

"A Harrowing scene!"
Bert tries disc harrowing.

Bert Churns the butter — After about 3 hours hard labour, the butter comes. He adds too much salt so pours in hot water to wash salt out. The butter washes out of the bung hole instead, to the great delight of his pet pig who wishes Bert would Churn every day!

Bertie had a little Pig, Its fleece was black as cork and every where where Bertie went that pig went too I think. Bert pig accompanies him rabbit trapping. Bert wondered why traps were sprung and no rabbits caught.

Bert sees nothing hard about ploughing but when he tried, he found the handles had a nasty habit of jumping up & bumping him in the ribs.

The Geese come home with their crops unusually full of our crops. Bert blames me for poisoning them all having scraped my paint palette in the backyard. He must have thought the geese had no more sense than he had.

1. Bert discovers a snake in the passage.

2. Bang! Lamp blows out.

3. "And darkness was upon the face of the earth." — and no matches.

4. We hunt high and low.

5. A week later.

GREAT SNAKES!"

No 6. The size the snake looked when B had stretched it on the wall & the stories of how he killed it were stretched still more.

No 1   No 2 It's real size

RED HEIFER

ALEC SMITH.
(Manager of
Balla Balla)

C H

E.B.H.

BLOSSOM.

Selling off our live stock at Cranbourne Market

DECR 1893. The red heifer leads us a dance where road is unfenced.

DECR 1893. Our last mail from the picturesque little Langwarren Post Office.
(Name afterwards changed to Pearcedale).
Funston's Store and post office.

THE SICK BUSHMAN.

Bert succumbs to the hardships and trials of country life
and declares that this farm will be his "qui-e-tus."
I discover him sitting in front of log fire enveloped in black selicia from
the studio darkroom

Bert collects Curios
to take to N.Z.

There was a little man
And he had a little gun,
And his bullets were made
of lead lead lead.
When he found it
wasn't loaded
And the "Laughing Jack"
exploded
You should have heard
the naughty words
he said said said.

"CRANBORNE MARKET."
Mond 11th DEC 93.
Selling off.
Old Neville & Billy Warchope.
Auctioneers.

The end of another chapter. The last days of our great farming enterprise.

"THE BUSH-BLACKSMITH."
(A long way after Landseer.)

Mond 11th DEC. 93 Shoe the grey mare for the trip to Melbourne, make an axe stuck in a log, do service for an Anvil & tack shoes on with french wire Nails.

Frid 17th DEC. 1893 Having sold off all our goods and run short of Stores we take the ferrits down to Bethune's paddock and get enough Meat to last us till we leave.

A sad moment.

DEC. 1893. Our farewell evening at Balla Balla Miss Johnson having joke with Bert - Telling his fortune.

DEC. 1893. The last of Warrain farm. We close the gate on the "old moke" and our Great Farming Enterprise.

SHOWING BOTANIC GARDENS "FARM COVE" SYDNEY, N.S.W. WITH CITY IN BACKGROUND, GOVT. HOUSE AND FORT MACQUARI ON THE RIGHT. MOND DECR 18TH 98.

MONDAY 18TH DECR 1898. Farm Cove. Sydney. Government house and Fort Macquarie on the right. Baths in foreground.

New Years day. 1894.

Maoris rubbing noses.

Decr 1898. On the Wellington & Manawatu Railway, on our way to Otaki to see Sister Lil and brother Jack Staveley.

Helen. C.H. Mable Bobbie. Bertie. Parika?

THE RESIDENCE OF MRS R.J. STAVELEY. OTAKI. N.Z.

Jan/ 1894. Stay a few days with Jack and Lil at Otaki. Bringing in the cow with the nephews and neices, Helen, Mable, "Bob" and Bertie. (The house was built by a Maori Chief.)

V

NEW ZEALAND AGAIN

After a brief stay with Lil and her husband, Bert and Charlie parted company. Charlie set out, as he says, 'for God knows where', his sketch-book always with him. He settled for a while in a Maori hut in the bush, but since the man he shared the hut with (Mad Harry, Charlie calls him) spoke only to the bread and cooking utensils and disappeared for days without explanation, loneliness drove Charlie to journey on. How he came to join the New Zealand Royal Artillery is a mystery, but in the same year (1894) we find him working on a vast sheep-station at Otakapo. But the life he had led with Bert in the Melbourne studio was seldom out of his mind. The new year saw him making his way across the Kaimanawa Mountains with the notion of setting up as an animal painter on the east coast at Wanganui, but he found the market already cornered by a Mr Fodor. The only brushwork he could get was repainting the lettering on the pediment of an hotel, balanced on the topmost ledge high above the street, which he wryly called 'High art in New Zealand'. By April he was back in Australia, helping to decorate the inside of Sydney Cathedral.

Bert and I part, he being useless in the country, remains in town while I strike out for God knows where. After walking many weary miles I arrive at a place called Akatarawa consisting of six settlers huts scattered over miles of mountain and bush on the fringe of civilization. No road, nearest store 12 miles away. No horse for miles, very few sheep and cattle except wild ones.

LIL.   JACK   E.B.H.   C.H.

Seeing no possible chance of following Art in Wellington I set off alone and make tracks for the Bush. Bert remains in town. A sad parting.

The long, long trail from Otaki to Akatarawa. Though tired and hungry with many miles yet to go. I sit down and sketch the beautiful scenery.

Mad Harry holds animated conversation with the bread and cooking utensils but never talks to me.

After travelling all day I arrive at Akatarawa hungry and exhausted, and find that the bush has been accidently set on fire. I sit and watch it nearly all night. Camp in a whare with mad bushman. only other companions being fleas and mosquitoes.

SETTLER'S LIFE IN NEW-ZEALAND.

Lunch on top of the mountain.

Returning to camp over the burnt logs utterly exausted.

Feb 9th 1894. All the settlers unite to burn off after mustering sheep & cattle. Soon miles of country are ablaze

Among the many dangers is that of huge burning logs crashing down the mountain side as the fire burns away the "Supplejack" Vines which held them up,

Lighting the bush in the Gully. Dangerous but unavoidable. almost certain death if the wind changes.

How we appeared after our narrow escape from being burnt alive.

Sunday morning. Wild pig hunting. On the hills of Akatareroa Sid Clendon up a tree

Sunday morning. Hair cutting "à la bushwhacker".

C.H.   SID.   VIC

Hard times after the bursting of the Land Boom.

"You cannot always tell a book by the cover".

I give an impromptu exhibition of trick shooting with revolver, rifle and shotgun. Shooting happened to be one of my favourite hobbies and I was in good form. The bushmen got the surprise of their lives.

Return to civilization. Too lonely and depressing shut in by mountains on all sides. Mac. Henry away for several days. No one to talk to; no stores.

Gun drill with 6 lb quick-firing Nordenfeldts.

C.H. (laying gun)   (Capt. Moorehouse)   (Serj M. Robinson)

D. Battery   C.H.   City Guards.

Morris tube match with City Guards. Wellington

Opening of Parliament. Wellington.

Opening of Parliament. Wellington. "D" Battery firing salute. 1894.

Sunday on the Station.

SUNDAY

"SHEPHERDING." SUNDAY. MORNING

C.H.

Sunday morning on Otakapo Station.

JIM. PATTERSON. C.H.

A mile race to the homestead after shepherding thousands of acres.
"Jim Patterson wins by a neck but I won the hearts of the station boys."

CORN.

Divine Service in the Woolshed Sunday night.
Minister rides over from Toorakina 9 miles.

FRED. ROWDEN. EDMUND. TUDOR. C.H. CHAS RUSSELL.

"The Evening hymn."

"MACINTOSH'S LAMENT"

Cameron walks over from Outstation with pipes and plays
MacIntosh's lament in front of the long room to the great delight of the boys.

Next morning the Station "wag" plays Macintosh's Lament while
docking lambs.

Shepherding in the back country

HOMESTEAD
SLAUGHTER HOUSE
OLD WOOLSHED
NEW WOOLSHED

Bringing sheep in to draft & house ready for Shearing.

Drafting ewes + lambs housing ewes ready for shearing.

Drafting ewes from lambs and housing ready for shearing.

The Shearing board. Otakapo Station (Heaton park)
These shearers get £1 to £2 a hundred.

B Low NP Low (Jen)
Edmd Tudor C Mc Russell
Fred Rowden C.H. Bert Mc Lean Scott Huddlestone Bob Craig
Jack Low. Yarnell

Jim Patterson

The twelve o'clock rush!

C.H. Bob Craig "THE DANCE OF THE SHEARERS."
Harp. Violin

Bob Craig plays Highland dances on the Violin & I accompany on
my harp. (They had never heard such music on the station before)
Two scotchmen, Cameron & Gear, also play bagpipes for some of the dances.

Otakapo Station, Rangitiki.

& Mr Huddlestone Shepherding.

Station boys going out after Cattle.

C.H.   F. Rowden   "Bob" Low   Chas Russel

"'Twas merry in the glowing morn among the gleaming grass, to wander as we've wandered many a mile
and blow the cool tobacco cloud, and watch the white wreaths pass, sitting loosely in the saddle all the while."
(GORDON.)

Yarding cattle from the back country.

A short cut home from Marton.

Fred Rowden gives the "rowdy dowdy boys" a lead over
fences by moonlight returning home Saturday night (or Sunday Morning)

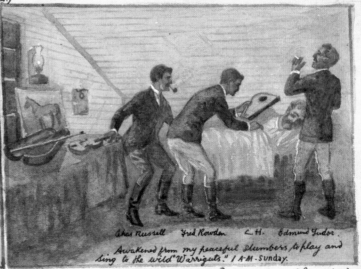

Chas Russell   Fred Rowden   C.H.   Edmund Tudor.
"Awakened from my peaceful slumbers, to play and
sing to the wild "Warriguts." 1 A·M·Sunday.

Sunday 1 A.M. The rowdy dowdy boys arrive at homestead
after Saturday nights spree in Marton! No more sleep for Chas!
"Come on Chas. Ups and downs, backwards and forwards!" &c.
(Their name for step dances.)

A LONELY MEAL.

Wake on Christmas morning to find myself alone. everybody
gone home including Cook, only hungry sheep dogs left.
nothing in the place to eat, no chance of getting any. find
4 biscuits tasting of Kerosene and a nest of bad eggs. no hope
of catching a horse on the Vast run. Prospects of a happy Christmas.

FRED LAUCHLAN.   MISS LOW.   MRS LAUCHLAN.
MISS FAULKELINE   C.H.   MISS LOW.

While pacing to and fro. wondering what to do for the next few days. Fred Lauchlan rides
over and after a chat and a laugh over my comical position invites me to spend the day with
him. So spend a Very happy day after all!

Christmas afternoon. Spearing fish in Lake Otakapo. in the old Maori Canoe.

Evening. Fishing for Eels by lamp light in Nursery lake.
A happy Ending to a Very pleasant Christmas day.

THE WANDERER SETTLES DOWN

Charlie was in Sydney and neighbouring Newcastle for about a year, while Bert made his way back to Melbourne. Once again Charlie joined him. The city was still suffering from the slump, but Charlie's life took a dramatic swing towards success. His drawing of the largest fire in the history of Melbourne was a scoop, and commissions began to pour in. There was a fellowship of artists, journalists, musicians and actors who used to meet in the evenings at Geary's Café and draw portraits of each other and of Bella the waitress.

But things were not so happy for Bert. His health was bad; his paintings had not had the success which Charlie believed they deserved. On 14 September 1904 (the sketch-book erroneously records the day as the 4th) Bertie shot himself on the beach at Sandringham, near to the plot of land he had bought for the dream-house which he had drawn for Charlie sixteen years before. Charlie's picture of the sunset of that day gives no idea of the full horror of the suicide.

In 1912 Charlie was living at Malvern and met a pianist called Thomas Kerr who owned land at Belgrave. Charlie bought two and a half acres from him, and set about clearing the site. He records the start of World War I, though he dates it a month too soon.

In November 1916 he brought his wife, Augusta Cecil, to live in the house he had built. He made a life-sized statue of Gussie to stand in the garden, and lived, as he said, a honeymoon life with her until she died in 1935. He lived on at Winscombe, painting occasionally, working in his garden, until his death on 28 November 1953.

Start with Lyons Potter and Wells.
Decorating Cathedral in Sydney.

Studying at the Sydney school of arts.

"The Judge said "You must n't swear in Court!"—

"Do you remember old Harry saying"—

"Oh! do stop."
(After a two hours laugh.)
I meet my good old friend Ted Bradford of the Minnie Casey in Sydney.
recalls some of our fokes even makes fun of the Wreck of the Wacarapa

"See you again tomorrow"—

Strange and unexpected meeting of
Tom Winters, ex-mate of the old Minnie Casey,
lumping on Circular Quay. Sydney.

MANLY BEACH.
Friday 5 April. 95. Bert arrives in Sidney from N.Z. en route for Melbourne
take a trip down the beautiful harbour to Manly. Relate past experiences
and future prospects as we have done many a time before.

Back to my old love.   Painting at Randwick.

Sept. 1895.
A Mr Mudge's Studio (Hamilton)   St Newcastle. N.S.W
(Thermometer 110° in shade for several days).

SUNDY 22ND SEPT 1895. A GHOST STOREY. Arrive at Newcastle from Sydney Saturday night. Attend Church with Mr & Mrs Mudge morning and afternoon, but remain at home alone in the evening. Sit in some darkness till 8.30, then go up stairs to get harp without a light. Get great surprise to see shaddow of a man on frosted landing window.

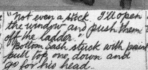

Shaddow on frosted window. "Hallo! Burglar, must have seen them go to church and did not know I was here".

"Two of 'em! They must have a ladder from the vacant land ajoining. My sixshooter at the bottom of my box not unpacked, no time to get that, no other weapon handy."

"Not even a stick. I'll open the window and push them off the ladder." Bottom sash stuck with paint pull top one down and go for his head.

A desperate dash at his head but it disappears though the body remains the same on the glass.

The mystery explained. Two men on verandah across the vacant allotment with a street lamp behind them quite unconcious of the scare they created.

My affection for Bert brings me once more to Melbourne as it had done from N.Z. in 1886. and from Leicester in 1889.

Leave Sydney Monday 13th April 1896. by 5.15 P.M. train. Arrive Melbourne Tuesday at noon.

Tues 14th Ap. 1896.

Find Bert in his Studio in Lombard Blds 16 Queens Street sitting at his easle, twirling his thumbs & waiting patiently for something to turn up.

Arrive back in Melbourne

Alec. Lang.   C.H.   EBH.   Bert. Walcott.

Start Studio in Premier Blds. next "Age" Office. Make the acquaintance of Bert Walcott; Alec. Lang; the Bishop Harold Power and others of the brush pushing and quill driving fraternity. We all agree that Melbs has not yet recovered from the boom. and it is mighty hard to make a living by art alone. no matter how tallented we may be.

I make another desperate attempt to make a living by art in Melbn although all the wiser ones have left for other parts.

Kept awake at night by the new bells of the G.P.O. clanging out "Hard times come again no more." "God bless the Prince of Wales." & "Home Sweet Home." (I wish God would bless the poor, struggling Artist and give him a home — be it ever so humble; — and a little prosperity. The Prince of Wales can take care of himself

LORDING'S STORE.

April 1896.   Painting the old Ferntree Gully Hotel from roof of Lording's store.

Sat 25th ap '96.

The old Ferntree Gully hotel.   * Shire hall & Lordings store on right. The shire pound in foreground.

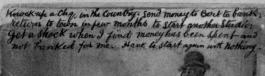

Knock up a Chq. in the Country: send money to Bert to bank. return to town in few months to start another Studio. Get a shock when I find money has been spent—and not banked for me. Have to start again with nothing.

The Tide Turns.

C.H.   Hirschberg.

Get order for as many Ships as I can paint. Just when I had given up the keys & things seemed hopeless.

Sunday 21st Nov.r 1897. 3 A.M. E.B.H. rushes up to Baroni Studios and wakes up Bert Walcott and me to tell us of the great fire at Craig Williamson's.

A few minutes later. Sketching the biggest fire in the history of Melbourne. There being no trains or trams running very few people about & no photographers. A.E.W. E.B.H. C.H. I had the only picture of it.

Monday 8 A.M. Rush around looking for another Studio having given up the keys and left the other one engage cab and at 9 A.M. remove to new Studio unpack materials and start drawing of the big fire. using a box for a table. Finish full page one by noon, run it down to Weekly Times office. Causes tremendous excitement. nobody else got a picture of it. W. Times just going to press but Editor holds it up for an hour while I make another drawing from across the river. Showing reflections in the water.

Great excitement at The W. Times Office. The biggest fire in the history of Melbourne. all the illustrated journals want a picture of it but owing to it occurring in the early hours of Sunday Morning no one else got it until the fire was nearly out.

Fred Kneebone   Sub Editor   C.H.   Mr Carrington Editor

Buckthorn Brunder

After pay day at the Weekly Times office, I "shout" the two Berts to the exhibition and a supper at Baroni Studios. They think it a great joke when I open my fat purse remembering the empty one of last week. Such is life among us bohemian artists.

Miss Geary
& Bella.   A. E. Walcott
                    Alec Lang. Bert. H.   C. H.
Our Snug Corner and happy nights at Geary's Café.

The tide turns. Fortune smiles; a tremendous rush of work comes in. My partner sells as many ships as I can paint. The first one takes me a week, but increase speed and improve methods till I can paint two a day 24 x 18" in water colour, correct in every detail to satisfy the officers and crews. Draw also for W. Times; Punch; Adelaide Critic and other journals. design advertisments and paint portraits of horses for Fred. Murphy, Roland Bishop and Sears, until nerves and health break down from overwork

Alec Lang.   AUG 98
Web Manager "Adelaide Critic."
Melbourne.

Bert Walcott.
Baroni Studios

Bella. Waitress

Dicky Vernon.   Aug
                        1898.
Son of Howard Vernon Actor
Stage name Prince.

Harry J. Weston
(Of the Southern School of drawing)
(Drawn by himself.)

The Red bluff Sandringham. Picnic point in middle distance.

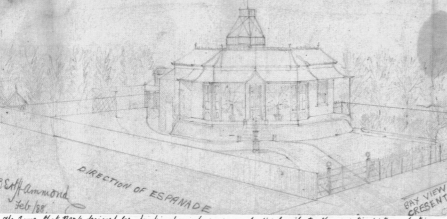

Sep. 4th 1904. After months of illness and worry, brother Bert passes out on the sands of his beloved Sandringham at sundown; another terrible shock to my already overstrained nerves.

My favourite brother from childhood, good natured and talented, who had planned such a happy future for us both at Sandringham; who had shared so many ups and downs, and been my sole chum for years, leaves me sad and lonely.

Fate willed that he should never live there — he could at least die there.

B. E. Hammond
Feb /88

DIRECTION OF ESPANADE

BAY VIEW CRESENT

The house that Bert designed for Sandringham where we were to live happily together, painting pictures, boating, bathing, fishing &c &c. The quiet, peaceful beach, with only an odd fisherman or so on it, far from the noisy city crowd, appealed to Bert. He wished to live and die there. He little thought of the bursting of the Land Boom and the terrible depression which was to follow in a year or two and upset all his plans.

The old man's bedroom

Back door through which the horse entered

To my studio

The biggest fright I ever had was one night at Dandenong when I thought an eccentric old man who rented the rooms under my studio had gone raving mad and was smashing things up with an axe and would soon be upstairs to murder me. He had been raving to himself all the evening after losing a court case and I could hear him mumbling till nearly midnight when I went into a sound sleep only to be awakened later by a terrific noise in the passage below; the old fellow shouting and cursing, things being knocked over; timber breaking; heavy stamping of feet; dogs barking in the street &c. Springing out of bed while still asleep I could not find matches, lamp, revolver or even the door. When the noise subsided I found the old man had left the back door and gate open and a horse had got into the narrow passage and in trying to back out had closed the door, got a fright and stampeded around the passage until the old man was able to open the door and let him out.

3

4.

↑ Dunn's Store
Coffee Palace ↗   MAIN ROAD, BELGRAVE.
1912.   Ry. Station ↘   EH

5.

AUTUMN. BELGRAVE MAY 1913.
COLE'S NURSERY.   The Pioneer of the district. (Now Lipscombe's)

My first glimpse of beautiful Belgrave.
The glorious view from Mr Kerr's verandah.   The sun rising
behind Black Hill.   The Mist drifting in the valley and the little
train winding among the hills on its way to Belgrave & F.T. Gully.
NOV. 2nd 1912.

Make a start to clear the land and build a hut out of the saplings
(Temperature 104° in shade)

Sat 14th March 1914. Ride up from Malvern to Belgrave 7 A.M. Terribly hot. Bush fires everywhere. Huge fire sweeps across from Alicanders property. Fighters check it at the railway line 50 yards from my hut. Sleep for first time under my own roof. Turn in 1 A.M. fully dressed and sleep with one eye open. Big trees crashing down all night, and flying sparks and burning leaves falling all round the hut.

Interior of hut. Everything made of bush timber.

Freddie Pitt comes along and gives me a hand to split posts for fencing my block.

24.

Sunday 5th July. 1914. New bungalow finished   Sleep for the first time under my own roof.   Clearing the land and laying out garden at "Winscombe" Main road. Belgrave.

1921.   SEVEN years later.   Showing additions to bungalow and lay-out of garden at "Winscombe" Main road, Belgrave.
                                                                                          (Named Tecoma in 1924)

1914 The passing of the coaching days. Mat Jankard starts a motor service in opposition to Wilson & Bowden's coach. The first motor service between Belgrave and F. T. Gully.

the Pfalz, built in 1913.
The Boorara is famous as the vessel
that provoked the first shot fired in
the Great War. As the Pfalz she
made a dash for the Heads from
Victoria Dock a few hours after war
was declared, but was stopped by the
Queenscliff Garrison, who shot across
her bows.

JULY 6th 1914. THE GREAT WORLD WAR STARTS

Thursday 6th July 1914. England declares war on Germany. Australia fires the first shot for England across the bows of the German Steamer Pfalz as she attempts to escape through the heads. And I am unable to go although I have been ready and willing since boyhood either to fight or as a war artist. Always interested in military affairs. A good horseman an crack shot, now the chance comes my ill health puts me out of it

Arthur Cecil. Mable. Gussie   C.H.

First glimpse of Miss A.F. Cecil.
Dinner at the Belgrave Coffee palace.

Mable & Arthur Cecil.

Gussie Cecil.   C.H.

Saty. 27th May. 1916. Mr Arthur R. Cecil comes to Belgrave to relieve Mr Stafford (school master) who has enlisted.   Invite him to my batchelor den. Sit over log fire and talk on various interesting subjects.   He is most entertaining. A great sense of humour. Good story teller & a wonderful mathematician. A good metallurgist and scientist. A clever all round fellow.

Sunday 11th June. 1916. Arthur brings his two sisters Gussie & Mable to Belgrave. Dine at Coffee palace and go for walk over Terry's hill after. Find Gussie as interesting as her brother.

Mond 17th July 1916.   Arthur Cecil rents "Waitarua" Terry's hill and brings sister Gus. up to keep house and give her a rest & a change.

C.H.   Gussie Cecil.   Arthur Cecil.

Tues 20th July. 1916.   My first evening with Arthur & Gus. at "Waitarua". Sit over the fire and listen to records on Arthur's phonograph. "The Mill in the forest." "Somewhere a voice is calling." "Absent." "A little love, a little kiss." and many others.

Friday 11th Aug. 1916. Our first walk to the Sherbrook falls.

The End

Mond. 11th Sept. 1916. Our first walk to Nathania Springs.   Gus names this view— PEACEFUL VALLEY.

View of The Patch from Old Monbulk Road.

26.

Friday 8th Sept. 1916. Our first walk to the reservoir.

SKETCH Book No 1

Wednesday 20th Sept. 1916. We make some remarkable discoveries
while looking through my sketch books. Gus thinks she
could be quiet happy & contented sharing this little cabin
of mine and taking care of a poor, sick, lonely artist.
I tell her she'll be sorry! but she is willing to try!
Brave old heart! So we marry & live happy EVER AFTER!